Dancing Dots

Brenda Eldridge

Dancing Dots

Dancing Dots
ISBN 978 1 76109 591 7
Copyright © text Brenda Eldridge 2023
Cover image: Marek Piwnicki from Pexels

First published 2023 by
GINNINDERRA PRESS
PO Box 3461 Port Adelaide 5015
www.ginninderrapress.com.au

Contents

Finding Light	9
Careless words	10
Learning to be still	11
Second-guessing	12
Importance	13
Saying too much	14
Getting the Message	15
Unique Silence	16
What was that word?	18
Memory	19
Not quite the Velveteen Rabbit	20
Does it have to be fanciful?	21
Swivel base	22
Perennial	23
The Art of Learning	24
Events	26
Passing Time	27
One Stitch at a Time	28
Alternative View	29
Brief Contentment	30
Sunny Afternoon	31
Waking Day	32
Changing Moods	34
So Little Change	35
No distraction	36
Shadow and Light	37
Winter Garden	38
Rain	40
Light	41
Moonlight	42

Blazing	43
Autumn Flames	44
Sun on the Foam	45
Iris	46
Picturesque	47
Drawn Curtains	48
Pacific Gulls	49
Hanging Out the Washing	50
Feeding Frenzy	51
Hyacinths	52
Heartsblood	54
Families	55
Bloodlines	56
Crying	57
Frailty	58
Rise Above it	59

Perhaps the emotion of time is precisely what time is for us.
Carlo Rovelli – *The Order of Time*

Finding Light

Self-doubt and sorrow had me held
in their iron grip for too many years so
I ventured out alone on my bike
and from the bridge I stood on
I looked for things to lift my gloom

Early morning sun cast lengthy shadows
across a building site of cleanly turned dirt
flashing on windows of industrious earthmovers

Overhead pearl-grey-breasted pigeons flickered
as they circled in a grey-blue clouded sky
grey water below made cheerful by white-tipped ripples
a solitary silver-grey dolphin made me smile

Red lighthouse now retired to the dock
surplus to requirements
pointed like a rude finger
having the last word

Buffeting wind made my hi-viz jacket
rustle and snap loudly
my hair dance and tangle
I noticed smoke coming horizontally
out of a chimney stack

Clouds were blown across the sun
I was left with the flashing lights of my bike

Lightness is everywhere if I look properly

Careless words

Too often we are careless with words
If only we had seen beforehand
how they would hurt and diminish

We react too quickly
don't pause to choose our words carefully
get impatient with those who refuse to be hurried

Are my words so important
they MUST be heard NOW

Were they worth the wounded look
the smile suddenly gone
shoulders slumping as if weighed down?

Does a gentle hug
a whispered 'I'm sorry'
erase the damage?
Do we ever fully recover?

Learning to be still

This morning the breeze is my companion
cool and fresh from the south
a pair of scruffy ordinary trees provide shade
from a sun not long risen
that sparkles hard and bright
off the tidal reach

I am learning to be still
in these quiet days

Second-guessing

A woman writing in a notebook
is like a man holding a fishing rod
both watching a river

No one second-guesses –
are they contemplating taking their own lives

There is evidence they are doing something
so all must be well

Importance

I sit and stitch for hours
a tapestry of someone else's design
watching a scene appear
beneath my darting needle and
coloured threads

I am not needed to create anything
I do not add something that was missing
I patiently follow the guide
and find satisfaction in the work

I am reminded of my importance –
without me this tapestry would not be done
but I am important to others too
making their lives a richer place

Saying too much

Books have gifted me visions I haven't actually seen
raised questions I would never have thought of alone

Is it the ocean or the sky that is darkest when
storm clouds obscure the stars?

I remember so clearly the book*
set on the southernmost area of South Island New Zealand
and the description of enormous seas
leaving me gasping and exhilarated –
me who dislikes being in a paddleboat on a shallow lake

I love how words can take me anywhere
fill my mind with images where anything is possible

I used to say that out loud
'Anything is possible
Most things are probable'
It often opened minds that were shuttered

I've said a lot of things
in the arrogant certainty of my own fears

---

* Adam Armstrong – *Song of the Sound*

Getting the Message

It wasn't easy to snatch moments of solitude
in the days when the needs of a young family
had an urgency that only children have
a wonderful immediacy
before they learn they must be patient
some never grasping
'All things come to those who wait'
and why should they
because it may come – but too late
a bit like wisdom

How many casualties must there be
before we get the message?

Unique Silence

Sometimes it isn't enough to just turn over
and go back to sleep
there is a unique silence at 3 a.m.
buttered toast and a cup of tea taste different
to the same had at breakfast

The waning moon little more than a mellow gold sickle
laidback as if enjoying the warmth
of the suns rays gently easing her above the horizon
has none of the attention-drawing glory
of a full moon riding proudly across the heavens
Jupiter shines not as brightly as Venus
but is her steadfast escort

It is said this is the time when our energy
is at its lowest ebb
the time we are most likely to drift from sleep
to the place of no return whatever we perceive that to be

For me 3 a.m. doesn't hold the same fears
as the harsh light of day
I can see things from other perspectives in the dark
Life more precious perhaps filled with unknown mysteries

I can't name constellations
much as I love the myths that have given them identities
stars that have a mesmerising twinkle as seen
in an old persons eyes
mischievous fun-loving
mocking our so-serious thoughts
inviting us to laugh as we dance from one to another

All things are possible at 3 a.m.
when you leave the warm comfort of your bed –
poems seems to write themselves
memories slip out into the open
calling softly 'remember me   remember when…'
and I do remember – and smile or shed a tear
because things are different at 3 a.m.

What was that word?

When we go out we notice Mustang cars
no particular reason beyond being easy to recognise
and seeming to make quite a statement of
'I am here look at me and envy'

A burnt orange one is often parked nearby
as if the owner works in a local office

A young man went striding past our home
nattily dressed with fancy earphones on
I started to say 'I bet he drives that…'
and my mind was blank

No, not a Ferrari – they are my favourite –
where was that elusive word
I kept silent hoping for divine intervention

It came after a few minutes
but by then the comment would have been pointless
and I still feel slightly anxious
about those blank moments

Memory

I've lost count of the weeks
since pelicans have perched on our posts

I have just glanced up
to see one flying silently by

What or who made me look up
at just that moment

The bird has gone from my sight
but I remember

It is memory that captures time
memories of my life
make me who I am

When illness or accident
deprives us of our memory
we lose ourselves

No wonder the accompanying terror
makes us lash out

Not quite the Velveteen Rabbit*

Years and years ago she asked what was my favourite colour
and shortly after gave me a yellow hand-crocheted blanket
a zigzag pattern that fascinates
as its pure wool warmth wraps me in cosiness
I can feel the care in every stitch

I should wash it –
the glow has become grubby
like the Velveteen Rabbit who knew he was real
because his coat had been made threadbare
by so much hugging by a small boy needing comfort

* Margery Williams – *The Velveteen Rabbit*

Does it have to be fanciful?

As I walked through the shallow waves
at the waterline enjoying a brisk breeze
and all that tumbling energy
I thought again of all the water on our planet

Was I being fanciful to imagine
if my feet were in the ocean here
then I was connected to all the oceans…
and the rivers that run into the seas…
and the countries where the rivers
had travelled on their journey to a sea…

If I read about different countries
I learn a little about their peoples
the way they live
things they believe in
how they know joy and pain
and I am sure they long for the same things I do…
a sense of belonging to something more
than I can see   hear   touch…
an eternal mystery

Swivel base

Once I dreamed of building a house
that stood on a swivel base
I wanted to be able to stand by the kitchen sink –
for me the heart of my home –
and watch the sunrise bringing a new day
filled with promise
then stand there again in the evening
to watch the sunset
and ponder the treasures of the closing day

At each end of the days and nights
I could watch cloud banners flying
skies filled with colours –
the unexpected rarity of green at twilight
be part of nature waking   sleeping
the soft call of birds – one last cheep
the first tentative welcome

Perennial

Words come drifting across my mind
and I have to stop and find out what they mean

This time I searched in a dictionary
and discovered perennial means
lasting an indefinitely long time
enduring
appearing again and again or year after year

I had been thinking in terms of flowers
that keep appearing in my garden
but it could be applied to many things
like empathy   compassion   love
and like growing plants
they need to be cared for
because not all things are like nasturtiums
thriving on neglect

The Art of Learning

Sitting in the cosy corner
on a dreary overcast winter afternoon
I can feel my brain stretch
as I try to take in concepts
of time and distance and the
smallest measurements possible of either

Past present future
without 'present' because before
I can say 'now' it is in the past

And all those dancing dots
that mean a rock isn't rock solid –
and the flowers I love are more dancing dots
the universe is dancing dots bumping into each other –
and they aren't really dancing dots
they are atoms or was it photons or…?
Oh dear

I put the book down on my lap
look out of the window
and time ceases to matter

On the horizon the heavy blanket of grey
has been magically lifted
and beneath it has been transformed
by the setting sun to a softly glowing golden yellow
an unseen artist adding moment by moment
orange and pink
which illuminates my mind and senses
and eases the angst of learning

* Carlo Rovelli – *The Order of Time*

Events

A glance at the right moment
silenced conversation
as we watched a lone swan
wings beating steadily
pass by arrow straight
with a clear sense of purpose…

I recalled from the book about time*
'The world is made up of events not things'
and tried to apply it to the swan –
both an event and a thing

I think I failed to grasp the concept
for more than the few minutes I was reading about it

It was as beautiful as the swan
but the memory of the swan is still with me
and I am still puzzled by time
and its possible absence

* Carlo Rovelli – *The Order of Time*

Passing Time

Is a day more precious as it reaches its end?
Does twilight gift the heavens a blessing
that touches a heart and sets a mind pondering?
Is time in this life more precious
when you know it will not last for much longer?

You see shapes clearer against the dark*
I read this once and felt the words settle within

I don't know if I fear the dark

I wonder when I watch the closing of a day
skies painted vivid colours
a fanfare to end a piece of music
if this were my last sunset
could I rejoice and be glad of the gift of life
or would I rail and fight against hard reality?

As always there are too many
and mostly unnecessary questions
better to treasure these moments
add them to my tapestry of life
know they are the golden threads
which remind me of its richness

* Elizabeth Webster – *A Boy Called Bracken*

One Stitch at a Time

Wearying of the complicated tapestry
that kept me occupied for months on end
when it was finished
I stopped doing embroidery

I gradually realised how much I needed to do
something with my hands
after a day working with words as an editor

I bought a simple cross-stitch kit –
and was soon reminded
with the gentle rhythm of stitching
how complex scarlet poppies are
with their delicate folds of colour
and I felt I was part of what was growing
beneath my fingers one stitch at a time

Alternative View

A white arum lily
whose regal beauty was not marred
by a tear through a petal

It was given an added dimension

At first glance another flower
on looking more closely
a flying kangaroo

Who said perfection is what we should strive for?

Sometimes beauty in the eye of the beholder
is more important

Brief Contentment

Many poems I have written
from indoors looking out
or indoors looking inward

After weeks of grey skies
today is bright and clear
only having lunch on the balcony not enough
I am lingering –

Being serenaded by intense exchanges
by squawking lorikeets
a noisy miner joining in with his strident call
there are other birds I could list…

Overlooking the sparkling tidal reach
sun warm through my cardigan
there is so much to enjoy
so much movement
as a passing breeze ruffles leaves

Sunny Afternoon

Three magpies are perched
on the rim of the bird bath
taking it in turns to sip

A fourth tries to work out
how to join them –
flutters up causing one
to drop to the garden

Numbers five and six
are strutting among the plants
when for no apparent reason
they have all taken off

A wattlebird preens carefully
one magpie returns
pecking away at the bark

The sun has broken through the clouds
tidal reach glitters
yellow tropicana lily glows

Outside all is movement
inside it is silent and still
the room filled with the lingering perfume
of pink lilies almost passed their best

A magpie sings on alone

Waking Day

What disturbs the gulls each morning?
One starts a harsh ragged sound
picked up by echoes or siblings
and soon the flock is in chorus

Do they welcome the day
the best way they know how?
No doubt their voices are not
the same to them as they are to me
I don't know their language
so I must not assume
their message is anything other than joyful

Is the impending sunrise
less glorious because it is hidden
among clouds that as yet
are not aglow with the pinks of a new day?
Is the tidal reach less alive because it seems still
surface broken rarely by circles made by blippy fish
the secret dwellers of the waters…

That I do not see smooth dorsal fins cutting the water
does not mean dolphins are not there…
I do not always see mosquitos
but feel their sting on bare arms and legs…

Noise and movement herald this day
even the clouds are dispersing to reveal pale blue sky
brightening light changes with each passing moment

Morning walkers   joggers   cyclists
cars rushing across the causeway
insistent bells at the train crossing

Still the gulls call to each other
joined now by melodious magpies
willy-wagtails and pigeons
add their voices – high and clear – low soft crooning

There is a pungent smell of dew-wet earth…

It is time to go time

Changing Moods

The tidal reach changes mood
as it reflects the sky

Still and silver-white in early morning and twilight
blue-green on a cloudless day
rippling black gold and silver at night
grey and lifeless beneath clouds

The apartment buildings across the water
are painted pale grey
but they soften to pink
with dawn colours
and their windows reflect fire in the sky

There is beauty in the old flour mill
the graceful arc of the bridge
making an interesting skyline

Small boats in the marina
tugging at their moorings –
perhaps longing for an open sea

And birdsong –
honeyeaters we don't see so much
in the garden these days
ever present magpies
gulls raucous not plaintive like the shags

They are all so full of life

So Little Change

February – month of unpredictable weather
has started cool and fresh
heavy clouds that will not bring rain for us
here on the plains

Sun sparkles glitter on the tidal reach
there must be movement – an undercurrent
even when it appears still

I relish these mornings
store them in my memory
against days to come
of high temperatures
gasping heat
sultry nights

A pelican in the far corner
someone said there were four dolphins
here a few days ago

So little changes here –
pandemics impinge on our freedoms
yet sitting here is timeless

Water   earth   sky

Easy to be still

No distraction

A breeze carries an incessant if muted roar
of traffic going over the bridge
not intrusive or I have grown accustomed
to its presence

A train rumbles over the trestle bridge
someone has started up a power tool
not to cut down soursobs*
I can still see them intact waving cheerfully to me
from across the water

None of that detracts from the simple pleasure
of sitting in the sun
watching the water racing along
impossible to tell if the tide
is come in or going out
until the posts are either
shortened or exposed

* *Oxalis pes-caprae*

Shadow and Light

Most of the day a tropicana lily stands in shade
its deep maroon leaves dancing
in every passing breeze

Tall sturdy-seeming stems
too easily bent and broken
by a strong gust of wind
denying fat spiky buds a life
as brilliant blooms of scarlet/crimson
a colour beyond mere words

By late afternoon when the sun
is low in the heavens
those dark leaves are changed
to bright orange and rust
each one a slightly different shape
different curves
different hues within each leaf
veins in sharp relief
a blend of strength and delicacy

Winter Garden

Air damp cold – morning sun barely warming my face
I knelt to pull weeds in the walled garden
thinning out wildly extravagant self-seeded nasturtiums
glorying in their vibrant scarlet blooms
among rich lush leaves
trimming exuberant convolvulus tendrils
that had threaded their way among everything else
trying hard to cover an elegant sculpture
there were too many seedling trees to tackle today –
everything was over the top…

Afternoon my favourite time and place
sitting in the cosy corner watching our other garden
with its background of the sparkling tidal reach
sun glaring through a few light clouds
sending shafts of light and flickering shadows
like a caress over my face
tropicana lily leaf made almost transparent
pale green and yellow with veins showing
its hidden life lines

A wattlebird squirms his way up inside branches
to find leftover crumbs
tossed over the balcony at lunchtime
then swooping across to the shrub
with masses of pale yellow trumpet flowers
providing afternoon delight
the lotus plant still has diamonds flashing
among its leaves – the sun has not dried them

Magpies warbling – can there be a more beautiful sound
in this country of oddities and squawking parrots

Slatted table top glistening still with overnight rain
seats leaning against it resting the winter away
making me remember how we have sat there
to have our breakfasts all through spring
summer and autumn

I do not wish time away
but look forward to having this start
to our day before too long

Rain

Steady drumming on our wooden balcony
drew me gradually from sleep
not heavy slashing or pounding
a gentle sound that soothed
as I drifted into wakefulness

In this corner of a dry country where I live
skies are huge and mostly clear
I have learned always to welcome rain
not complain at another day of grey

We have planted Australian native bushes
to attract the birds
I have forsaken growing my own vegetables
they needed so much watering for small return

I need rain as much as the earth does
I seem to have wept most of my tears
raged all my helpless storms
have found inner calm
and I let the heavens weep for me

Light

Great billowing clouds of gleaming white
with dark grey hearts
can make all here on earth seem small

Fingers of light pouring out
in all directions
all encompassing
illuminating
lifting willing hearts and spirits

Light reflected on moving silver water
offers a sign of redemption for us
a reminder there is more to our world
than our questing minds can envision

Moonlight

Before dawn she soared in darkness
bright white
shining cold like the morning

Lowering to the west
she mellowed before my eyes
softening to rich cream and growing larger
as the sky lightened
her reflection rippled on the tidal reach

She became almost transparent
against a backdrop of early morning pink
I didn't reach for the camera
there was something sacred in these moments
not to be cheapened or sensationalised
I must trust to memory

I knew that time had passed
without me being aware of it

Did I lose those minutes?
Are they somewhere or simply in the past?
Are they remembered because of the moon?

Endless questions

Surely I can learn to accept these gifts without asking…

Blazing

When I hear the word blazing
my thoughts go to roaring fires –
safe within the confines of a fireplace
or a well-tended bonfire in a garden
or roaring out of control through the wild

So I was surprised when I looked out of the window
to see Venus blazing in the night sky

No other word would do

There was no thought of warmth or fire –
she blazed with cold glittering light
which may be due to my poor eyesight
or our cleaner atmosphere since travel
has changed with the pandemic

Perhaps this is how she looked
to the Ancient Ones
before we messed it all up

What a beautiful reminder I have had

Autumn Flames

Beneath a clear blue sky
Australian blue-green foliage
was intermixed with foreign trees
wearing their autumn splendour

Yellow gold russet crimson maroon
flames of colour
that lifted my senses
enriched my life
without the fear of a bushfire

Sun on the Foam

Ocean waters swirl around my ankles
cold making my feet burn

Overhead an icy blue sky with puffy clouds
a full moon fading fast

Sun still low pouring over my shoulder
finding bubbles of rainbows
in gleaming white foam

Snowy gull puddling in the wet sand

All is movement as a cold wind sneaks
through my clothes

Iris

Pure colours shine in a perfect arch
Iris, goddess of rainbows
connecting heaven and earth

Mythology to some who do not want
mystery in their lives
preferring to be discontent
with gloom-laden facts and figures

I need to dream the ocean is still clean
is still all shades of blue
unsullied by pollution
that I can be refreshed by a surging tide
white foam filled with rainbows
and not all is being destroyed by modern living

Picturesque

Sitting sheltered by sand dunes I see
silver-blue sea calm before me
a white-sailed yacht bobbing

There is the smell of damp grasses
made redolent by night dew

Mounds of seaweed like sleeping seals
without their barely hidden ferocity

I can witness these things
and write down what touches
my senses
my imagination

Drawn Curtains

A blustery sparkly morning
white-capped waves rolling in
gleaming when a reluctant sun
shone on them gifting them extra magic

Sand clean and windswept
harsh on my face
I could taste salt on my lips

A passing angel touched my shoulder
I looked out to sea
and as if a curtain was being pulled aside
a rainbow appeared

A perfect arc from sea to sea
and in seconds the curtain was drawn again
the rainbow was gone –
leaving a heart-warming memory

Pacific Gulls

Overhead a glossy white Pacific gull
fish or crab in its beak
chased by two youths
still in their brown plumage

They soared low over the sand
then veered to the dunes
huge
silent

Hanging Out the Washing

A man-made breakwater
was an ideal place for cormorants to gather
for a debate on the state of the world
where the best fish are running
or simply to hang out their wings
like washing in the breeze
enjoying the camaraderie for a short time
before diving back into the seething waters

Feeding Frenzy

The usual calm surface of the tidal reach
is a mass of ripples –
not single ones that might indicate a dolphin or two
these heralded a gathering of hungry birds
shags   silver gulls   cormorants   terns

They swooped to one spot then suddenly lifted
to splash down only a few feet away
one moving the rest following

On and on they went
and I wondered what shoal of fish
might be beneath the surface that tempted them so
and was there any significance
that they did it earlier this morning
and again now in the late afternoon

Hyacinths

The unmistakable smell of hyacinths
sent me wandering down memory lane
and I wrote a book about my childhood*
recalling it through the passing of seasons
rituals within my family and our village

Visiting our local garden centre recently
I was astonished to see hyacinths
in full flower but bending over
as if they were exhausted
by being forced too early to perform

I came home and looked in the terracotta pot
which had stood as if empty for months –
there were two small humps in the mulch

Over a few days I watched as strong green nubs appeared
once again sending me tumbling back in time
not even needing their perfume as a companion
for I knew this would come

My hyacinths are doing their own thing
they will grow inch by inch
thick succulent leaves – a spire of buds
that will open
reminding me of
swaths of bluebells in springtime beech woods
I feel the anticipation…
what colour will they be?

Here is all the magic of childhood
in one small terracotta pot
a very long way in time and distance
from where my roots began…

* Brenda Eldridge – *Flower Child*

Heartsblood

I don't know what colour heartsblood is
I only know when I look into
the petals of this exotic deep crimson lily
that is what I think of

Five petals with crimped edges have opened slowly
in the quiet warmth of this room
releasing a fragrant perfume
that makes me pause each time I walk past

Flowers know that they are not to be hurried
they will flourish only when they are ready
then like some special gift they send an invitation

Was there something so very important to be done
that smelling the roses or – in this case – the lily
had to be rushed

Isn't the reminder of our heartsblood
pumping steadily giving us life
good enough reason to pause…

Families

A fully grown little grebe
bobbed like a cork on the tidal reach
then in a flash dived beneath the surface
coming up moments later
looking slightly comical
as if it had surprised itself

It looked far too small to be alone

I hoped it had family close by
or perhaps it was expecting a mate
and they would make a raft of a nest
have tiny babies
life doing what life does best…
continuity

My hopes were realised
as some days later I saw two more
not huddled together
yet clearly their own little flock

Much like families everywhere
not always together
no constant reminders needed
as each member goes forth
builds a life of their own
knowing the singing of love
keeps them all forever as one

Bloodlines

My four sons have an Irish father
and an English mother
they all grew up here in Australia
with mixed – and history could suggest
contentious – blood
running through their veins

What is passed down through the gene pool?

Why does this one have his father's sense of humour
at the same time
reminding me of my dad when he laughs?

Why do some grandsons remind me of my mother
and my older brothers
and others their Irish relatives

I made a collage of six generations of my family
from my paternal grandparents
to my great-granddaughter
and there are the eyes
the shape of a mouth
similar features that leave no doubt
we are all connected

Crying

My brother said recently
When you hear of my demise don't cry for me
I've had an eventful life
dodged death once or twice…

I said
No I won't cry for you but I will cry for myself

I accepted our solitariness long ago –
over fifty years living on opposite sides of the world –
but I cherish thoughts about my brothers
and their children
my sons
my grandchildren
for they are all part of who I am

Frailty

I have no difficulty seeing and feeling nature's blessings
constant yet ever-changing

My heart is full of human frailty
also constant and ever-changing

One moment I can laugh
am brave joyful
another moment tears
gather in my eyes
and all the beauty is surrounded by rainbows
beauty of a different kind

I weather moments of outrage
ride the storms of anger
knowing I can change nothing
I tire myself with thoughts
that can only go round and round
achieving nothing
no new perspective unseen before
and I yearn for stillness

Rise Above it

I promised myself I would not go back
not even to hold her hand
so she would not die alone

The call of a life I had longed for
which came to me late
was so precious
I did not want to go back
to a pain-filled past

As long as I have a memory
I will have
the gems she gifted me
helpful hints to live a calm life by

The most often used?

Rise above it darling
Just rise above it…

and I do

as she did

www.ingramcontent.com/pod-product-compliance
Lightning Source LLC
Chambersburg PA
CBHW071036080526
44587CB00015B/2642